Searchlight BOOKS™

What's Cool about Science?

Discover

Forensic Science

L. E. Carmichael

Lerner Publications ◆ Minneapolis

Content Consultant: Ashley Hall, PhD, Assistant Professor, Forensic Science, Department of Biopharmaceutical Sciences, University of Illinois at Chicago

Lerner Publications Company
A division of Lerner Publishing Group, Inc.
241 First Avenue North
Minneapolis, MN 55401 USA

For reading levels and more information, look up this title at
www.lernerbooks.com.

Library of Congress Cataloging-in-Publication Data

Names: Carmichael, L. E. (Lindsey E.), author.
Title: Discover forensic science / by L. E. Carmichael.
Description: Minneapolis : Lerner Publications, [2017] | Series: Searchlight books. What's
    cool about science? | Audience: Ages 8–11. | Audience: Grades 4 to 6. | Includes
    bibliographical references and index.
Identifiers: LCCN 2015044358 (print) | LCCN 2016007120 (ebook) |
    ISBN 9781512408058 (lb : alk. paper) | ISBN 9781512412871 (pb : alk. paper) |
    ISBN 9781512410662 (eb pdf)
Subjects: LCSH: Forensic sciences—Juvenile literature. | Criminal investigation—Juvenile
    literature.
Classification: LCC HV8073.8 .C3755 2017 (print) | LCC HV8073.8 (ebook) | DDC
    363.25—dc23

LC record available at http://lccn.loc.gov/2015044358

Manufactured in the United States of America
2-44072-21202-4/18/2017

Contents

Chapter 1

WHAT IS FORENSIC SCIENCE?

Forensic science is the use of scientific knowledge to solve crimes. When criminals commit crimes, they leave behind evidence. That evidence could be a victim's wound, a broken window, or a bullet.

All crimes leave evidence. What are some examples of evidence?

Forensic scientists interpret these clues. They uncover the details of the crime. With the right evidence, scientists can identify a criminal even if no one saw the crime take place.

Forensic scientists carefully examine crime scenes.

Unlocking the Evidence

One of the earliest forensic scientists was Edmond Locard. In 1910, Locard opened the first science lab dedicated to fighting crime. He solved mysteries using tiny clues. He looked at dust, hairs, threads from clothes, and similar traces.

LOCARD CONTINUED HIS RESEARCH ON FORENSIC SCIENCE INTO THE 1960S.

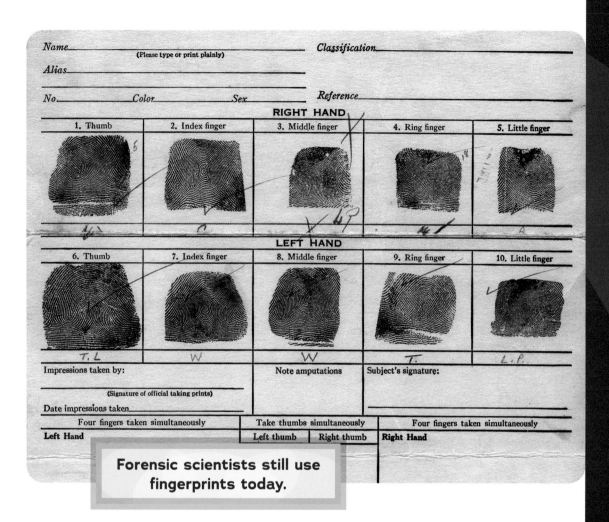

Name				Classification	
(Please type or print plainly)					
Alias					
No.	Color		Sex	Reference	

RIGHT HAND

1. Thumb	2. Index finger	3. Middle finger	4. Ring finger	5. Little finger

LEFT HAND

6. Thumb	7. Index finger	8. Middle finger	9. Ring finger	10. Little finger

Impressions taken by:		Note amputations	Subject's signature:	
(Signature of official taking prints)				
Date impressions taken				

Four fingers taken simultaneously	Take thumbs simultaneously		Four fingers taken simultaneously
Left Hand	Left thumb	Right thumb	Right Hand

Forensic scientists still use fingerprints today.

Locard's fellow scientists focused on other kinds of clues. Some found ways to test for poison in a victim's body. Others discovered that every person has unique fingerprints. Scientists found ways to track the weapons criminals used.

Criminals use gloves and other tools to try to avoid leaving evidence.

Today's forensic scientists still use these methods. But criminals are crafty. They may switch to new poisons. They can wear gloves to hide their fingerprints. They may throw away tools or weapons used in a crime.

To stay a step ahead, forensic scientists are always finding new ways to uncover evidence. Some use specially trained dogs to track scents. Others study how bugs can be used to determine a person's time of death. Scientists also use cutting-edge DNA science to identify criminals.

Forensic scientists use microscopes to study evidence that is invisible to the naked eye.

Forensic scientists are experts in finding and studying all kinds of evidence. Science makes it possible for them to help bring criminals to justice.

Taking measurements of bullet holes can provide forensic scientists with important evidence.

Fire Forensics

Setting fires is a crime called arson. Gasoline burns very easily, so criminals often use it to start the blaze. Finding gasoline in a burned building is good evidence of arson.

Burning gasoline reacts with wood, paint, and furniture. This creates a complicated chemical mixture. In 2014, forensic scientists invented a computer program that studies these chemicals. It can find tiny traces of gasoline. The program makes proving arson much easier.

Some firefighters have forensics training to investigate arson.

Chapter 2

CADAVER DOGS AND LABRADORS

A man is missing. The police suspect murder. To prove it, they must find his body. The woods behind his house are a good place to look.

Police close off areas that are under investigation so trained dogs can work. What are these dogs known as?

POLICE LINE DO NOT CROSS

The police send trained dogs into the brush. The dogs are known as cadaver dogs. They are commonly Labradors or German shepherds. They sniff for the scent of death.

Dogs have a much better sense of smell than their human companions have.

After death, bodies decompose. This means they break down and rot. During decomposition, chemical reactions take place. The reactions produce new chemicals with strong smells. Living people have unique scents, but all dead bodies smell alike.

DECOMPOSING BODIES BREAK DOWN IN PREDICTABLE WAYS.

Some cadaver dogs can find bodies underwater.

Cadaver dogs recognize the smell of dead bodies. Their noses are at least 10,000 times more sensitive than human noses. Cadaver dogs can find bodies hidden decades ago. They can even find bodies buried underground. These dogs are powerful helpers for forensic scientists.

Finding a Grave

Back in the woods, one dog lies down and barks. It is not tired of searching. It is alerting its trainers. It has found the scent. Cadaver dogs are trained to alert this way. Jumping or digging could destroy important evidence. The dog's trainer rewards it with a favorite toy. It has found a body and helped solve a crime.

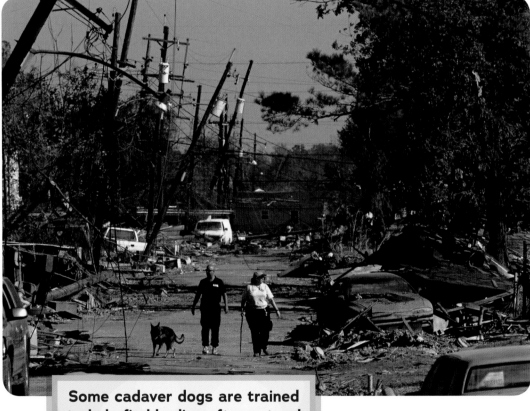

Some cadaver dogs are trained to help find bodies after natural disasters, such as hurricanes.

Teaching a Dog to Sniff

Before they can look for bodies, cadaver dogs are trained and tested. Trainers rub human body smell on a toy. Then they play with the dog. The dog learns that body smell and playtime are connected. Next, trainers hide the scent. The dog must find the scent to get the toy. Cadaver dogs often train using real human blood. Some trainers use fake human scent made by scientists instead.

Cadaver dogs train for several months before joining a forensics team.

Cadaver dogs almost never make mistakes. But sometimes the spot they find does not have a body. The smell has traveled away from the grave. This happens when chemicals sink into the soil or dissolve in rain.

Rain can wash away the smells from decomposing bodies.

CADAVER DOGS CAN HAVE TROUBLE
FINDING A BODY IF THE SMELL HAS
SPREAD TO OTHER AREAS.

Scents may travel more than 0.5 miles (0.8 kilometers) from the grave. Dogs can find smells, but they cannot tell where the smells originally came from.

LABRADOR can. LABRADOR stands for "light-weight analyzer for buried remains and odor recognition." It is a handheld machine that can smell. LABRADOR detects thirty chemicals produced during decomposition.

LABRADOR contains twelve sensors that detect chemicals.

LABRADOR was created by the Oak Ridge National Laboratory in Tennessee.

LABRADOR also measures the scents' strength. Scents are strongest where the body is buried. Forensic scientists can follow the scent trail straight to the grave. LABRADOR has found more than one hundred hidden bodies since it was introduced in 2010.

Chapter 3

BODIES AND BUGS

In the woods, searchers find a woman's body. Her forehead is bruised. Did she fall while hiking, or did someone hit her? To find out, police take the body to a forensics lab for an autopsy.

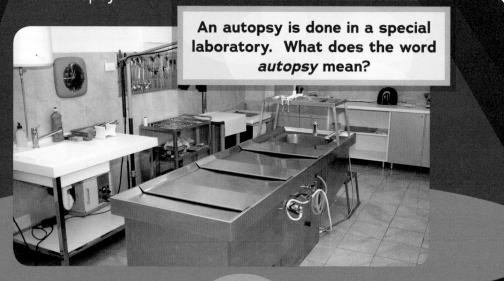

An autopsy is done in a special laboratory. What does the word *autopsy* mean?

Autopsy means "seeing with your own eyes." During an autopsy, scientists study a victim's body inside and out. They look for natural causes of death, such as disease. They also look for evidence of a crime.

AUTOPSIES CAN PROVIDE IMPORTANT
EVIDENCE ABOUT HOW A PERSON DIED.

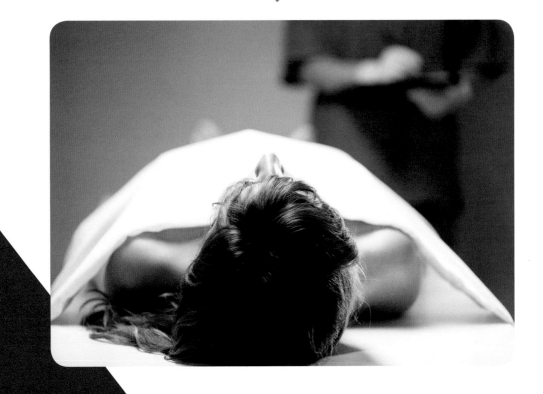

Injuries are one type of evidence. Scientists try to match injuries to weapons. They compare the shape of stab wounds to the shape of knives. They match grooves on bullets to the ridges inside guns.

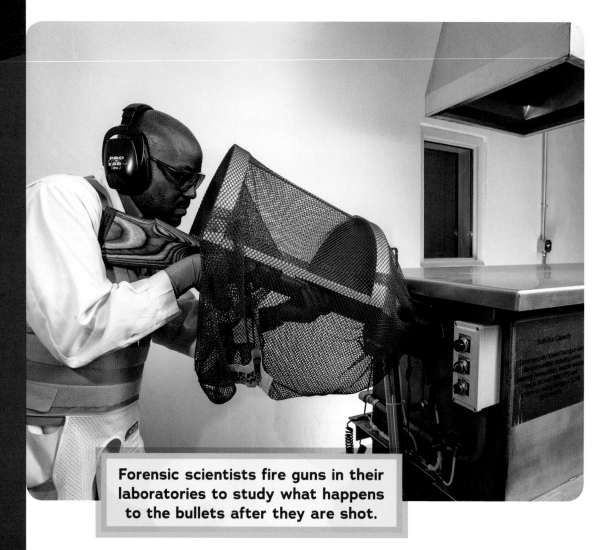

Forensic scientists fire guns in their laboratories to study what happens to the bullets after they are shot.

Once a body is found, forensic scientists gather evidence from the area around it.

In the woman's case, the evidence is clear. Her injury did not come from an accident. She was murdered.

Time of Death

To catch the killer, police need to know when the murder happened. Estimating the time of death is very difficult. Insects can help.

Animals of all sizes are eaten by insects as they decompose.

Many types of insects eat dead human bodies. Each kind prefers a different stage of decomposition. Some like dry, old bodies. Others prefer fresher bodies.

Studying flies and other insects near dead bodies can help forensic scientists estimate the time of death.

Blowflies can smell a body within fifteen minutes of death. They lay their eggs on the victim. Maggots hatch and feast on the body. They eventually grow into adult blowflies. Scientists know how long this process takes. They measure the age of the insects on and around the body. Scientists count backward to estimate when blowflies first arrived. This shows the rough time of death.

YOUNG FLIES, KNOWN AS MAGGOTS, ARE COMMON INSECTS FOUND ON DECOMPOSING BODIES.

Body Farms

Forensic scientists study decomposition at body farms. People who want to help forensic science agree to donate their bodies to these farms when they die. They make this donation to help advance forensic science. Scientists bury some of the bodies. They place others in sunlight or under shady trees. Then they watch how the bodies break down. In 2015, a scientist at a body farm in Texas noticed that scorpion flies find fresh bodies before blowflies do. If the discovery is confirmed, it could help scientists better estimate time of death.

The first body farm opened at the University of Tennessee in the 1980s.

Chapter 4

DIGGING INTO DNA

During the autopsy of the woman found in the woods, scientists found evidence of her killer. The criminal left clues at the crime scene. They are skin cells trapped under the woman's fingernails.

Skin cells can provide evidence of a crime. What chemical in cells can help identify a murderer?

The woman scratched her killer before she died. These cells are an important discovery. Forensic scientists can use a chemical inside the skin cells to help identify the murderer. This chemical is known as DNA.

Scientists can also collect DNA from objects that a criminal touched.

DNA Matching

DNA stands for deoxyribonucleic acid. It contains the chemical instructions that make a person unique. It is found in almost every cell in the body. This includes cells in the skin, muscle, hair, bones, and blood.

DNA exists in a twisted ladder shape known as a double helix.

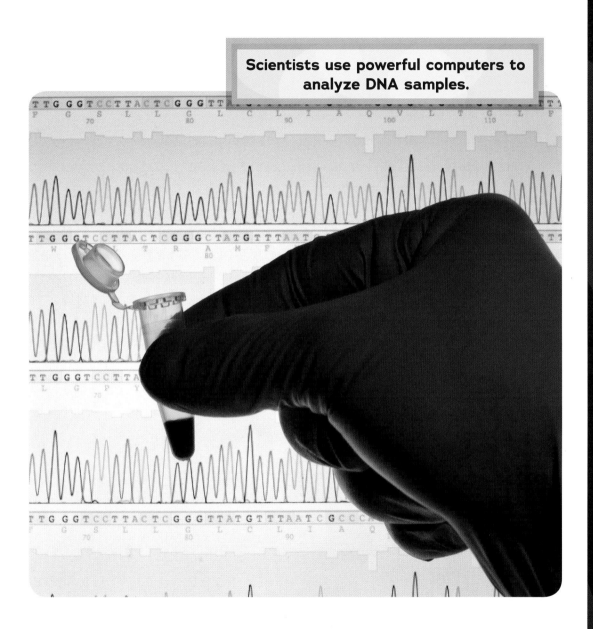

Scientists use powerful computers to analyze DNA samples.

Some parts of DNA are called genes. Genes control how the human body works and looks. Some genes are very similar between people. Other parts of DNA vary.

Cracking the Case

Back in the lab, scientists test the DNA from the killer's skin cells. Police have three suspects. They collect DNA samples from each one. Scientists compare these samples to the DNA from the crime scene. Only one person's DNA matches. He is likely the killer. Science has cracked the case.

Detectives can collect suspects' DNA samples using cheek swabs.

Telling Twins Apart

Identical twins have identical DNA fingerprints. This can make it difficult to prove which twin committed a murder if one of them is a suspect. But in 2015, scientists discovered a way to tell twins apart. Differences in living habits or environment can affect twins' DNA. In one twin, a gene might switch on. In the other twin, it stays switched off. These switches change the patterns of DNA. By comparing these patterns, scientists can now figure out which twin left DNA at a crime scene.

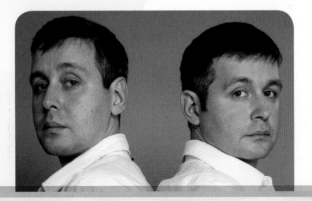

The new method of studying DNA means that criminals won't get away with crimes just because they have an identical twin.

Science Fiction, Forensic Fact

Today's forensic labs can do things Edmond Locard never imagined. And today's forensic scientists keep inventing new ways to unlock evidence. Forensic science remains one of the best ways to solve crimes.

From tiny DNA samples to entire cars, forensic scientists study all kinds of evidence.

AROUND THE WORLD, FORENSIC SCIENTISTS ARE USING THEIR SKILLS TO BRING CRIMINALS TO JUSTICE.

Unlike witnesses, evidence never lies. It does not forget or become confused. Forensic evidence is factual evidence. Forensic scientists will continue fighting crime for years to come.

Glossary

arson: the criminal act of setting a fire on purpose

autopsy: examining a person's body after death to learn about how he or she died

cadaver: the body of a person who has died

cadaver dog: a dog trained to locate dead bodies

cell: a tiny building block that makes up a living thing. Skin, hair, and blood are made of different kinds of cells.

decomposition: the breakdown of a human body into smaller pieces after death

DNA: deoxyribonucleic acid, a chemical in the body that contains the instructions that make each person unique

evidence: physical objects used to reconstruct what happened during a crime, also called clues

forensics lab: a space in which forensic scientists do their work

witness: a person who saw a crime take place

LERNER

SOURCE™

Expand learning beyond the printed book. Download free, complementary educational resources for this book from our website, www.lerneresource.com.

Learn More about forensic Science

Books

Shea, John. *DNA Up Close*. New York: Gareth Stevens, 2014. Explore genes and DNA. Learn what DNA is for, how it works, and how scientists use it.

Sutherland, Adam. *Police Forensics: The Crimes, The Clues, The Science*. Minneapolis, MN: Lerner, 2011. Learn about different types of forensic science and read interviews with experts and stories about real cases.

Townsend, John. *Forensic Secrets*. Mankato, MN: Amicus, 2012. Explore an overview of forensic science and its use in real crimes.

Websites

Dialogue for Kids: Crime Scene Investigation
http://idahoptv.org/dialogue4kids/season12/csi/facts.cfm
Check out TV episodes, articles, and books about forensics.

FBI Kids Page
https://www.fbi.gov/fun-games/kids/kids
Learn everything you ever wanted to know about forensics and the Federal Bureau of Investigation.

Kids Ahead: Crime Scene Investigation
http://kidsahead.com/subjects/3-forensics
Read articles on forensics and learn forensic activities you can do at home.

Index

Photo Acknowledgments

The images in this book are used with the permission of: © Linda Steward/iStock.com, p. 4; © Ivan Bliznetsov/iStock.com, p. 5; © Maurice Jarnoux/Paris Match/Getty Images, p. 6; © belterz/iStock.com, p. 7; © Manuel Faba Ortega/iStock.com, p. 8; © aefoto/iStock.com, p. 9; © Sean Justice/Corbis, p. 10; © Charles Schug/iStock.com, p. 11; © Maxiphoto/iStock.com, p. 12; © Shannon Stapeleton/Reuters/Corbis, p. 13; © Lipowski Milan/Shutterstock.com, p. 14; © Christopher Furlong/Getty Images, p. 15; © Nader Khouri/Contra Costa Times/KRT/Newscom, p. 16; © pawprincestudios/iStock.com, p. 17; © karamysh/Shutterstock.com, p. 18; © Aaron M. Sprecher/EPA/Newscom, p. 19; Image courtesy of Oak Ridge National Laboratory, U.S. Dept. of Energy, pp. 20, 21; © Picsfive/Shutterstock.com, p. 22; © KatarzynaBialasiewicz/iStock.com, p. 23; © Richard T. Nowitz/Science Source, pp. 24, 31, 36; © Fotosmurf03/iStock.com, p. 25; © samuiboy/iStock.com, p. 26; © imv/iStock.com, p. 27; © CreativeNature_nl/iStock.com, p. 28; © Kenneth Murray/Science Source, p. 29; © IS_ImageSource/iStock.com, p. 30; © SilverV/iStock.com, p. 32; © damerau/Shutterstock.com, p. 33; © Leah-Anne Thompson/Shutterstock.com, p. 34; © meo_photo/iStock.com, p. 35; © PeopleImages/iStock.com, p. 37.

Front Cover: © Michael Donne, University of Manchester/Science Source.

Main body text set in Adrianna Regular 14/20.
Typeface provided by Chank.